IMAGES of America

PISGAH INN

In this photograph, taken between 1923 and 1926, Pisgah National Forest Inn guests find respite beside its massive native-rock fireplace. Behind the gentleman seated at the hearth, and out of view in this image, a grand piano invited musicians to add soft melodies to the relaxed atmosphere. (Courtesy UNCA.)

On the Cover: The D.H. Ramsey Library Special Collections at the University of North Carolina at Asheville (UNCA) provided this photograph, taken some time between 1923 to 1926, of the original Pisgah National Forest Inn constructed around 1919 on land leased from the US Forest Service. (Courtesy UNCA.)

IMAGES
of America

PISGAH INN

Marci Spencer

ARCADIA
PUBLISHING

ISBN 978-1-4671-0503-3

Published by Arcadia Publishing
Charleston, South Carolina

Printed in the United States of America

Library of Congress Control Number: 2019954920

For all general information, please contact Arcadia Publishing:
Telephone 843-853-2070
Fax 843-853-0044
E-mail sales@arcadiapublishing.com
For customer service and orders:
Toll-Free 1-888-313-2665

Visit us on the Internet at www.arcadiapublishing.com

To my husband, Dr. John P. Spencer, who joined me on all of my research journeys and still asked after each chapter's manuscript draft to "read me a story."

Contents

Acknowledgments

When crews built the Blue Ridge Parkway between Shenandoah and Great Smoky Mountains National Parks, the scenic roadway passed within a few miles of my childhood home near Asheville, North Carolina. My dad, Max Garland Lance, frequently accepted its irresistible invitation to tour its natural and cultural history. On many weekends, the family loaded in his Ford station wagon to explore the Craggies, Mount Mitchell, Shining Rock Wilderness, Graveyard Fields, and especially Mount Pisgah and the Pisgah Inn. In December 1985, dad led us on a hike from Pisgah Inn to our South Asheville home, following George Vanderbilt's old Shut-In Trail that roughly parallels the parkway. Thank you, Dad, for hearing the call of the mountains and taking me with you—for helping me recognize life's natural rhythms and the past and present history that affects them.

I sincerely thank the patient individuals who answered my endless questions in hundreds of emails, phone calls, and interviews during my research. Their knowledgeable insight helped shape and preserve this recorded history. Thanks for the professional guidance from Paul Sisco of the American Chestnut Foundation as well as historians George Ellison, Bill Hart, and Dan Pittillo. I appreciate the supportive assistance from the archivists at the Old Buncombe Genealogical Society, the National Park Service (NPS) Blue Ridge Parkway (BRP) Archives, and the Buncombe, Henderson, Haywood, and Transylvania Counties library systems. Pisgah Inn staff members and their relatives added personal life experiences to the text.

My fondest gratitude extends to Sharon Corn, Walt Weber, Jere Brittain, NPS/BRP curator Jackie Holt, Debbie Maxwell Sammeth, Carolyn Allen, Amy Coy, and Teri Troitino Connelly for proofreading the manuscript. Many thanks for the beautiful map and drawing of George Weston created by Ken Czarnomski and the illustration provided by Michael Worsham and Shelby and Lydia Wallace. I am most appreciative of Pisgah Inn's managers for over 30 years, Bruce O'Connell and his mother, Phyllis O'Connell Prevost, who offered their support, inspiration, personal stories, and historical documents to make this project possible. Thank you, Arcadia Publishing editor Angel Hisnanick and others in the publication process, for your professional wisdom.

INTRODUCTION

Follow Pisgah Inn's dining room host to the round table in the far corner.

Face the large dining room windows offering spectacular scenic views. Cast your eyes over Pisgah National Forest, the first national forest in the East established under the Weeks Act, which allowed the US government to purchase lands for protection. Take extra moments to outline distinctive landmarks like Black Mountain, Funnel Top, and Looking Glass Rock. Imagine rock climbers ascending the steep rock face of Looking Glass Rock near the former site of George Vanderbilt's ladder. In the early 1900s, crews built a wooden ladder up the bold mountainside to offer Vanderbilt's Biltmore Estate guests a grand view from the top. Peregrine falcons, saved in the 1980s from an endangered status, now successfully nest on its narrow cliffs.

Scan the deep valley below Pisgah Ridge, where prolific pink blooms of laurels, phlox, and other wildflowers encouraged early settlers to call their valley home the "Pink Beds." Here, in 1898, a German forester, Carl Schenck, requested George Vanderbilt's permission to organize America's first school of forestry. Today, the US Forest Service preserves the historic site as the Cradle of Forestry in America.

From the corner table, turn your attention to the right along Pisgah Ridge. There, in 1919, George Weston and local labor built the original Pisgah National Forest Inn, constructing the complex in the Adirondacks mountain lodge style popular at the time. The rustic Kalmia, Chewink, Chinquapin, and Treetops Cabins provided additional accommodations for visitors at the resort. Over 300 transplanted native wildflowers highlighted a one-acre garden near the entrance to the main lodge. In the early 1900s, wealthy summer travelers from the sultry southern coasts and crowded large cities sought the healthy physical and emotional benefits of leisure time at the Pisgah National Forest Inn on this high ridgeline in the Western North Carolina mountains. Throughout the 1970s and 1980s, preservationists, historians, and sentimental citizens led a passionate campaign to preserve the original structures. Even though decay, economics, and a need for updated accommodations for Blue Ridge Parkway visitors forced its removal, fond memories still linger.

In the Pisgah Inn Dining Room, who joins you for dinner? Residents from nearby cities and towns like Brevard, Asheville, Hendersonville, Waynesville, and Candler who take an afternoon escape on the Blue Ridge Parkway and dine at the inn regularly? Are there long-distant travelers who are driving the parkway from end to end? Overnight lodge guests from Ohio, Michigan, Florida, Texas, or even foreign countries like France or Australia? Are couples celebrating an anniversary? Are there relatives joining an overdue family reunion? Have former staff members returned to reminisce about their brief life at the top?

For decades, the Pisgah Inn Restaurant has hosted organized groups, such as student foresters learning scientific forestry management practices in the neighboring national forest, conservationists who campaigned for a new national park on the border of Tennessee and North Carolina, and advisors from Holland training workers at the new rayon processing plant in nearby Candler, North

Carolina. College students and professors came to study native wildflowers in the local forests and in a rare high mountain bog in the Mount Pisgah Campground. Businessmen, politicians, writers, artists, Lady Bird Johnson, private citizens, and others also came, seeking inspiration and restorative peace at the Pisgah Inn retreat among nature's grandeur.

After dinner at Pisgah Inn, walk the historic trail beneath the dining room windows. The trail, now designated as part of the Mountains-to-Sea Trail that stretches across the state of North Carolina, follows a portion of an early route that guests traveled to access the original Pisgah Inn. An easy trail from the north end of the Pisgah Inn parking lot leads to the former site of George Vanderbilt's private Buck Spring Lodge. To burn more calories, locate the Mount Pisgah trailhead near the Buck Spring Overlook and climb this prominent peak. Enjoy the 360-degree view that has enticed visitors for over 100 years.

Leave Pisgah Inn and drive north on the Blue Ridge Parkway, eyeing the master workmanship of stonemasons who constructed the parkway's signature tunnels. Turn onto Highway 151 at the parkway's Elk Pasture Gap, where the US Forest Service enclosed a wildlife preserve around 1918 to reintroduce elk and buffalo in the new Pisgah National Forest. Continue a windy, scenic drive on Highway 151 to the quiet, pastoral community of Hominy Valley. Highway 151 traces the historic dirt roadway built in the early 1900s by George Vanderbilt to access his Buck Spring Lodge built on Pisgah Ridge.

A driver turning left out of the Pisgah Inn parking lot heads south on the Blue Ridge Parkway past the National Park Service Mount Pisgah Campground and the US Forest Service historic Fryingpan Fire Tower. At the Blue Ridge Parkway junction with US 276, a traveler curves right onto US 276 to visit the rural communities of Cruso and Canton, where several local residents who helped build and maintain Pisgah Inn and Vanderbilt's Buck Spring Lodge raised their families. A left turn off the parkway onto US 276 offers adventures in Pisgah National Forest—backcountry hiking trails, campgrounds, picnic areas, historic sites, and gorgeous waterfalls.

In this book, Images in America: *Pisgah Inn*, a photographic journey retraces the history of this beloved mountain resort, located in the Blue Ridge Parkway's Mount Pisgah Recreation Area—one of the most visited mountainous areas in Western North Carolina. Although the original 1919 Pisgah National Forest Inn is gone, its visual memories, captioned with personal stories and archived descriptions, can now be revisited in this preserved, published record. The current Pisgah Inn, built in the 1960s, maintains the historic traditions of the former lodge. Next to the inn on a grassy overlook, find a rocking chair offering a warm invitation. Relax. Allow some mental time for a nostalgic trip of a treasured past. Immerse yourself in nature's rejuvenating beauty and leave renewed, anticipating a return visit.

One

Pisgah National Forest

During the late 1800s, George Vanderbilt began buying thousands of acres in Western North Carolina to build his Biltmore House and Estate, including land in Buncombe, Transylvania, Haywood, and Henderson Counties. He named 80,000 acres of his wooded areas Pisgah Forest. After his death in 1914, his widow, Edith Vanderbilt, sold Pisgah Forest to the US government. This acreage became the core of the Pisgah Ranger District of Pisgah National Forest. (Courtesy UNCA.)

George W. Vanderbilt II was the grandson of the wealthy shipping and railroad businessman Cornelius Vanderbilt. Between 1889 and 1895, George's inheritance funded the construction of the largest private residence in the United States. Vanderbilt bought large tracts of land in Western North Carolina to become his estate. By 1895, he owned more than 100,000 acres. (Both, courtesy UNCA.)

Vanderbilt's Biltmore House and Gardens, located near Asheville, North Carolina, covered nearly four acres. Richard Morris Hunt, the architect of the 255-room mansion, had designed mansions along Fifth Avenue in New York City, a portion of the Metropolitan Museum of Art, the pedestal for the Statue of Liberty, and other historic architectural projects. To design his gardens and surrounding forests near the Biltmore House, Vanderbilt hired landscape architect Frederick Law Olmsted, who had designed Central Park in New York and the landscaped grounds around the US Capitol Building in Washington, DC. (Courtesy UNCA.)

In 1891, Vanderbilt hired a forester, Gifford Pinchot, an American trained and educated in the forests of France, to manage his vast forestlands. At Vanderbilt's request, Pinchot surveyed the lush mountainous region west of the Biltmore Estate and suggested that Vanderbilt purchase what became his Pisgah Forest. Above, Gifford Pinchot is standing on Pisgah Ridge below Mount Pisgah around the late 1800s to early 1900s. (Both, courtesy UNCA.)

Later, Gifford Pinchot left Vanderbilt's services to work as a consulting forester in New York. He directed the US Division of Forestry in 1898, and by 1905, Pinchot became the first chief of the new US Forest Service. Pinchot's friend and fellow conservationist, Pres. Theodore Roosevelt, visited the Biltmore House and the Battery Park Hotel in Asheville around 1902. From the hotel's balcony, Roosevelt gazed toward Mount Pisgah and the surrounding mountains and said, "These are indeed the greatest east of the Rockies!" (Courtesy UNCA.)

From Asheville and the Biltmore House, Vanderbilt could gaze at Mount Pisgah, a distinctive 5,722-foot peak on the distant horizon. In 1885, he paid Sen. Thomas Clingman $800 for 300 acres on Mount Pisgah. In his early career, Clingman established his law office and home in Asheville and explored the surrounding mountains. A bitter disagreement with Dr. Elisha Mitchell ensued over the measurement of the highest mountain in the East, now known as Mount Mitchell. Today, Clingmans Dome in Great Smoky Mountains National Park honors the name of the senator. (Courtesy Pack Memorial Library.)

Around 1895, Carl Schenck, a German forester, came to the Biltmore Estate to replace Pinchot. Before Pinchot departed for New York, the two men camped on Pisgah Ridge, discussing the forest's future. While working for Vanderbilt, Gifford Pinchot (pictured here) had initiated the first scientific forestry management plan in America. Carl Schenck would open the nation's first forestry school in Vanderbilt's Pisgah Forest. (Courtesy UNCA.)

In 1898, Carl Schenck opened the Biltmore Forest School, the first structured forestry education program in the United States. Schenck and his professional instructors taught winter classes in Biltmore Village with field studies on the Biltmore Estate. In the summer, the Biltmore "boys" attended classes in a one-room schoolhouse in a wide, flat valley called the Pink Beds. (Courtesy Library of Congress.)

Under the direction of Carl Schenck, Biltmore Forest School students built over 200 miles of roads and trails, planted trees, learned scientific forest management methods, and practiced wise timber harvesting measures. Over 300 foresters graduated from Biltmore Forest School. Overton W. Price, a 1902 graduate, became the deputy chief of the US Forest Service under its chief, Gifford Pinchot, around 1905. (Courtesy UNCA.)

In a 1905 progress report, Carl Schenck discussed the forest management achievements, the harvest profits, and the improved natural environments in Pisgah Forest. However, his suggestion to dam Davidson River to generate power for a mill, to build a lake at the Pink Beds for an electrical power plant, or to create a picturesque lake near Looking Glass Rock never happened. Around 1909, Vanderbilt released Schenck from his employment at Biltmore. (Courtesy UNCA.)

In the western United States in the late 1800s, the federal government had set aside land out of the public domain to protect as forest reserves. However, private owners held much of the land in the East. Logging companies who held thousands of acres had left the land denuded and eroded. By 1911, Congress passed the Weeks Act, allowing the federal government to purchase land from private owners to set aside as protected national forests. (Courtesy Mountain Gateway Museum.)

By 1913, George Vanderbilt wanted to sell Pisgah Forest to the US government. Officials from the Biltmore Estate negotiated with representatives from the National Forest Reservation Commission at Vanderbilt's mountain retreat, Buck Spring Lodge, at the base of Mount Pisgah, but the two parties could not reach an agreement. (Courtesy NPS/BRP.)

After George Vanderbilt's death in 1914, his widow contacted the US government about buying Vanderbilt's Pisgah Forest. Overton Westfeldt Price, a family friend and member of the prominent Westfeldt family of Fletcher, North Carolina, helped Edith Vanderbilt negotiate the sale of 80,000 acres to the US Forest Service. She wrote the secretary of agriculture, requesting that the USFS protect Pisgah Forest to provide public recreation and to "perpetuate my husband's pioneer work in forest conservation." (Courtesy UNCA.)

In October 1916, the US Forest Service combined Vanderbilt's Pisgah Forest and other large tracts of land to establish Pisgah National Forest, the first national forest in the East created under the Weeks Act. Verne Rhoades, a graduate of the Biltmore Forest School, became Pisgah's first supervisor. (Courtesy UNCA.)

Pisgah Ridge in the Balsam Mountains culminates with Mount Pisgah, a grand, alluring peak that lends its name to the national forest. Four North Carolina counties meet at the top and claim its beloved slopes. Haywood County, formed from part of Buncombe County and named for state treasurer John Haywood (1755–1827), lies north and west of Mount Pisgah. To the north and east is Buncombe County, formed from parts of Burke and Rutherford Counties in 1791 and named for a Revolutionary War hero, Col. Edward Buncombe. Pisgah's south and west slopes occupy Transylvania County, formed from parts of Jackson and Henderson Counties in 1861. Its name joins two Latin words meaning "across the woods." Flanking Pisgah to the south and east is Henderson County, formed in 1836 from part of Buncombe County and named for chief justice of the state supreme court Leonard Henderson (1773–1833). Ancestors of the Eastern Band of the Cherokee Nation called Mount Pisgah Elseetoss and Pisgah Ridge Warwasseeta. (Courtesy UNCA.)

West of Asheville, the broad basin of Hominy Valley welcomed visitors to climb its stunning masterpiece looming on the horizon, Mount Pisgah. Around 1911, George Vanderbilt built a road from this valley to the top of the ridge. The one-way, curvy dirt road terrified one Florida driver. He told Ranger William Cogburn, stationed at the top, "If you get me off this mountain, I'll give you my car!" (Courtesy UNCA.)

After 1916, the USFS operated Vanderbilt's Pisgah Motor Road as a Stoney Fork roadway entrance to the new Pisgah National Forest at the head of Hominy Valley. Note the sign that instructs motorists to ascend and later descend during assigned periods each day. The state widened and paved this road several years later as NC 112. Today, that roadway, NC 151, joins Elk Pasture Gap on the Blue Ridge Parkway. (Courtesy UNCA.)

In 1916, the Southern Forestry Congress voted to honor George Vanderbilt at the Stoney Fork entrance of the new Pisgah National Forest. USFS supervisor Verne Rhoades moved a seven-foot-tall boulder from the Pink Beds. The embedded bronze plaque read, "This portion of 83,398 acres was formerly Pisgah Forest established by George W. Vanderbilt in 1891 and the earliest example of forestry on a large scale on private lands in America." (Right, courtesy UNCA; below, courtesy Biltmore Estate Archives.)

By 1920, two rock columns held a concrete arched banner engraved "Pisgah National Forest," welcoming visitors arriving near Brevard, North Carolina. A bronze bald eagle perched on top. Around 1941, when the Department of Transportation widened the road now known as US 276, officials dedicated a new memorial at the entrance. By 1953, the bronze eagle went missing and never returned. (Courtesy Transylvania County Library.)

Pisgah Motor Road climbed the mountainside from Stoney Fork in Hominy Valley to a gap in the ridgeline, now known as Elk Pasture Gap. When the USFS purchased the area in 1914, wildlife officials established the Pisgah Gameland Preserve to protect wildlife and reintroduce buffalo and elk. Sponsored by the American Bison Association, a project to reintroduce buffalo to the new Pisgah Gameland Preserve began January 1919. (Both, courtesy UNCA.)

Transported by rail from New Hampshire to the Hominy Valley, six crated buffaloes and the association's escort, Martin Garretson, were met by USFS supervisor Rudolph Dieffenbach at Hominy Valley's Southern Railway train station. The animals were moved by wagons up the Pisgah Motor Road to the elk pasture at the Pisgah Gameland Preserve. (Courtesy UNCA.)

While USFS supervisor Verne Rhoades attended Officer's Training Corps and served as a captain in World War I, Rudolph Dieffenbach (USFS) organized the buffalo reintroduction project. A Mr. Grath (right), with the American Steel and Wire Company, offered his expertise to help construct effective fencing for the elk and buffalo. By 1930, though, the elk and buffalo had either died, escaped, or were killed by locals. (Right, courtesy UNCA; below, courtesy Transylvania County Library.)

Between 1895 and 1903, George Farrington Weston had worked for George Vanderbilt as a superintendent of his pig, poultry, and dairy farms on the Biltmore Estate. In 1917, Weston requested a concession permit from the new Pisgah National Forest. He wanted to build a mountain inn on Pisgah Ridge south of Vanderbilt's Buck Spring Lodge. The USFS approved the plan and offered Weston a 30-year lease. While the construction of Pisgah Inn progressed, the USFS managed

wildlife, restocked fish, fought fires, and built campgrounds. Around 1920, the USFS completed the new Flat Laurel Gap Campground, now known as Mount Pisgah Campground. South of Weston's guest lodge, a photographer captured USFS supervisor Verne Rhoades, innkeeper George Weston (seated second from left), and James Scott and Tom Gill of the USFS camping beside Pisgah's first fireplace at Flat Laurel Gap. (Courtesy Transylvania County Library.)

In June 1916, a local newspaper stated that USFS officials of the new Pisgah National Forest invited visitors to come fish, explore, and picnic in Western North Carolina's new "beautiful playground." It boasted rushing streams, long-range mountain views, and gorgeous waterfalls, like Looking Glass Falls. The forest service also invited the public to apply for a five-acre property lease to build camps and summer homes in the new national forest. (Author's collection.)

By 1933, Pisgah National Forest received assistance for the restoration of visitor facilities from the Civilian Conservation Corps (CCC). Pres. Franklin D. Roosevelt created the "Tree Army" to provide incomes and training for economically strapped young men and their families while tending the nation's forests. In Pisgah, the CCC built campgrounds, fish hatcheries, fire towers, and rock bridges and helped staff the US Deer Farm. (Courtesy UNCA.)

Two

Buck Spring Lodge

On Pisgah Ridge in 1896, George Vanderbilt of the Biltmore House and Gardens built his personal mountain retreat, Buck Spring Lodge. When his widow, Edith, sold Vanderbilt's Pisgah Forest to the federal government around 1914, she kept the mountain retreat. Thirty years later, George Weston would build his guest lodge, Pisgah National Forest Inn, on Pisgah Ridge about one mile south of Buck Spring Lodge. (Courtesy NPS/BRP.)

In the late 1880s, Vanderbilt joined his forester Carl Schenck and his landscape architect Frederick Law Olmsted Jr. at Buck Spring Gap at the base of Mount Pisgah. On a small knoll about 5,000 feet in elevation, they chose the site for the construction of the original lodge complex, which included a main lodge, a stable, a kitchen–dining room, and a two-story ranger's quarters. (Author's collection.)

Local loggers and family-owned sawmills from the surrounding valleys provided massive chestnut, yellow poplar, and hemlock logs to build the lodge. Oxen pulled heavy loads up a six percent–grade, 3,000-foot-ascent over a commuter road from Cruso, North Carolina, to Buck Spring Gap. Local stonemasons built foundations, rock steps, and retaining walls from native stone. (Courtesy UNCA.)

On file at the Blue Ridge Parkway Headquarters, a taped interview with William Cogburn Jr. and George Vanderbilt's grandson George Cecil mentioned the Millers, the caretakers of Buck Spring Lodge around the 1930s. The couple lived in the ranger's quarters across the road from the main lodge. The Millers remembered a chandelier with winged angels. A handcrafted wooden staircase led to a balcony and a well-stocked library. Red velvet curtains and chairs decorated the dining room. A massive wood-burning fireplace provided comfort and warmth in both the lobby of the main lodge as well as the dining area. Smaller fireplaces heated the bedrooms. (Both, courtesy NPS/BRP.)

According to William Harrison Cogburn Jr. (1927–2019), his father, William Sr. (1880–1953), was born one-quarter of a mile northwest of the Buck Spring Lodge site. William Sr.'s father, Freeman Hardy Cogburn Sr. (1856–1934), lived near Cruso at the headwaters of Pisgah Creek and raised apples near Mount Pisgah. Family lore affirms that Hardy Cogburn charged Vanderbilt a toll to cross his apple orchard to access the Buck Spring Lodge. Hardy allowed Carl Schenck to build a road across his property to haul materials up to the lodge construction site. After the lodge was completed, the staff transported provisions for Vanderbilt and his guests up this rugged four-mile route. This photograph was taken on August 1, 1961. (Courtesy NPS/BRP.)

William Cogburn Sr. caught fish to feed Vanderbilt's surveyors. "Paid to go fishing!" chuckled William Jr. "Dad thought he'd died and gone to heaven!" After working as a water boy for lodge construction crews, Cogburn Sr. became an assistant ranger. On November 4, 1910, the *Asheville Citizen* reported, "Biltmore Ranger Is Killed by Huntsmen." While patrolling Vanderbilt's boundary line on horseback near Slate Rock Creek off Yellow Gap Road (now FS Road 1206), Ranger Clayton "Clete" Davis and his assistant, Will Cogburn Sr., heard gunfire. A bullet hit Davis in the abdomen. Cogburn rode three miles to Buck Spring for help. He immediately returned with a wagon and rescuers only to find Davis struggling to crawl the two miles toward his home, where he later died. Biltmore Estate superintendent Chauncey Beadle and Dr. W.D. Hilliard of Asheville arrived at the lodge, where estate employees formed a posse to leave "at once to search for the slayer. A thorough beating of the woods commenced." The suspect, a Mr. Kearns of Mills River, surrendered himself, claiming he mistook the ranger for a deer and accidentally shot him. By 1912, Vanderbilt hired Cogburn Sr. to replace Ranger Davis. (Courtesy Dave Landreth.)

In 1898, George Vanderbilt married Edith Stuyvesant Dresser. Together, they entertained friends on summer retreats at the mountain lodge. Ladies in long skirts joined gentlemen in fine suits on steep hikes to the top of Mount Pisgah for a sunset. From the lodge, the cleared open knoll offered distant views. Sheep and occasionally a dairy cow grazed nearby. Today, the Blue Ridge Parkway divides Vanderbilt's former Buck Spring Lodge property. Vegetable gardens, tennis courts, and croquet fields occupied the fields now known as the Mount Pisgah Picnic Area. (Courtesy UNCA.)

The year that George and Edith Vanderbilt married, Carl Schenck began offering classes at the Biltmore Forest School. In the summer, instructors taught forest management classes in the one-room schoolhouse in the Pink Beds. The surrounding Pisgah Forest became their outdoor classroom. At times, the students camped in the high-elevation forests on Pisgah Ridge, near the Buck Spring Lodge. (Courtesy UNCA.)

On the 10th anniversary of the Biltmore Forest School, Carl Schenck held a three-day Forest Festival for politicians, loggers, businessmen, and foresters to educate them about his scientific forestry practices. Horse-and-carriage rides toured guests through the Biltmore Estate and Pisgah Forest. Biltmore students provided demonstrations on forest regeneration projects. Schenck invited festival participants to climb Mount Pisgah before "spending the night at the Buck Spring Hunting Lodge amongst the stars." (Courtesy UNCA.)

Carl Schenck visited the Vanderbilts and their friends at Buck Spring Lodge. After crews completed its construction, Schenk invited Gifford Pinchot to visit the new lodge at the base of Mount Pisgah, where the two of them had camped together years earlier. Pinchot regretfully turned down the invitation, writing in a letter dated July 5, 1897, "Pressures from work will absolutely prevent me from getting to the Biltmore until this fall." Later, locals became fascinated with the mountain

retreat as well. In a letter written to the Biltmore Office, Joe E. Johnson of Canton wrote, "I wish to visit the famous Vanderbilt Buck Spring Lodge on Mount Pisgah. I have been informed that a pass from the Biltmore Office was required. Wishing to comply, I beg leave to ask you for a pass for a party of four." (Courtesy NPS/BRP.)

According to George Vanderbilt's grandson George Cecil, Biltmore Estate superintendent Chauncey Beadle designed the curvy single-track Pisgah Motor Road to climb an even grade up the mountainside. "The Westons built the Pisgah Inn around 1919 south of Buck Spring Lodge," said George Cecil at a 2015 public gathering in the renovated Buck Spring Lodge cabin known as the Honeymoon Cottage. "People would come up the Pisgah Motor Road but not necessarily to see the Buck Spring Lodge. Pisgah Inn was a great place to get a Sunday lunch." Buck Spring Lodge rangers communicated with gatekeepers in the valley at Stoney Fork. Uphill traffic climbed the mountain in the morning; downhill traffic traveled in the afternoon. When the Pisgah National Forest opened the road for visitors to the new national forest, owners of Pisgah View Ranch moved the former gatekeeper's booth to their property and offered it as guest accommodations. In 2019, North Carolina governor Roy Cooper signed a bill to purchase and develop the 1,600-acre, family-owned Pisgah View Ranch as a state park. (Photograph by Christi Worsham; used with permission from George Cecil.)

In 1911, Vanderbilt paid $50 for the combined one-room Stoney Fork School and Meetinghouse built in the 1800s in Hominy Valley. A construction team disassembled it and transported the materials up to the Buck Spring Lodge site via the Pisgah Motor Road. There, the two-bedroom, one-bath cabin became the Honeymoon Cottage. (Courtesy UNCA.)

After George Vanderbilt suffered fatal complications from an appendectomy in March 1914, his widow, Edith, sold 80,000 acres of Pisgah Forest to the US government. She chose to retain about 470 acres surrounding the Buck Spring Lodge. Before her marriage to Sen. Peter Gerry around 1925, she spent many weeks at the mountain retreat. When she died in 1958, the mountain lodge passed to her grandson George Cecil. (Courtesy NPS/BRP.)

In the 1930s, landscape architects began discussing the idea of constructing a scenic parkway between the Shenandoah and Great Smoky Mountains National Parks. By 1946, officials planned to route the parkway along Pisgah Ridge and raised questions about the future of the Buck Spring Lodge, the Pisgah Inn, and other Pisgah-area developments. Initially, the government offered to purchase George Cecil's Buck Spring Lodge property, but Cecil declined the offer. Parkway leaders had another thought: They suggested that Leslie and Leda Kirschner, owners of Pisgah Inn (pictured below), invest $12,000 to upgrade the Buck Spring Lodge water and sewer system and manage it as part of their Pisgah Inn resort. (Above, courtesy NPS/BRP; below, courtesy UNCA, Ball Collection.)

After the discussion of many options, George Cecil sold Vanderbilt's mountain lodge to the state government in 1959. The state later transferred the property to the National Park Service for construction of the Blue Ridge Parkway. (Note the park ranger on the upstairs balcony.) Preservationists and historians suggested that the park service turn the main lodge into a Blue Ridge Parkway visitor center or museum. (Courtesy NPS/BRP.)

Financial and other concerns forced the decision to raze Buck Spring Lodge. In 1961, bulldozers and heavy equipment practically erased the Vanderbilt era from the base of Mount Pisgah. George Cecil was there that day. A man on a bulldozer pointed to the cornerstone of the main lodge with the initials "GWV" engraved in it. "Do you want that?" he asked. Without hesitating, George Vanderbilt's grandson George Cecil claimed a treasured piece of Buck Spring Lodge history. (Courtesy Pack Memorial Library.)

George Cecil also retained the former Stoney Fork Schoolhouse/Honeymoon Cottage and moved it several times. It became a guest cabin at his home at Lake Toxaway and later a playhouse for his grandchildren. Today, Biltmore Company's gated community in South Asheville, The Ramble Biltmore Forest, preserves the little 1800s cabin for garden club meetings and other events. In the front yard, flowers surround the boulder engraved with "GWV." (Courtesy Christi Worsham.)

Located today next to the entrance road to the BRP Buck Spring Overlook, Vanderbilt's 1890s springhouse is the only remaining original structure on site. Hidden behind a dense cover of rhododendron beside the Blue Ridge Parkway, its well-fitted chestnut log walls resting on a rock-solid foundation make it larger than most period farmstead springhouses (9 feet by 11 feet). Oak shakes cover the gabled roof. (Author's collection.)

Robert (Bob) Allen dismantled the ranger's quarters at Buck Spring. In the 1960s, Allen built a log cabin with the materials for him and his wife, Phyllis, near Royal Pines in South Asheville. Allen's father, Ernest, and his brother Bill had worked as Biltmore farm managers. Allen had driven a truck for Biltmore Dairy. Bob and Phyllis Allen lived in the cabin until he died in 1990. Upon her death in 2014, their descendants offered it to the Biltmore Estate. Today, the former ranger's home serves as the Outdoor Adventure Center in Antler Hill at Biltmore. (Both, author's collection.)

In 2004, Walt Weber and the Carolina Mountain Club, which maintains the Mountains-to-Sea Trail along Pisgah Ridge, met with Blue Ridge Parkway officials to propose clearing the former Buck Spring Lodge site and its foundations to preserve the area as an interpretive historic site. Parkway officials agreed to a proposed plan. In November, 60 volunteers cleared decades of overgrowth from the lodge site, uncovering foundations, retaining walls, and stone steps. (Both, author's collection.)

Parkway administrative issues stalled the 2004 preservation plans at the Buck Spring Lodge site. Over the years, vandals had cut and defaced the Blue Ridge Parkway's original exhibit there. Around 2015, however, project leader Walt Weber (left), George Cecil (center), and BRP superintendent Mark Wood (right) hosted a ceremony dedicating a new interpretative Buck Spring Lodge exhibit. Annually, Carolina Mountain Club members clear the area of overgrowth. Today, the BRP manages the 29-acre Buck Spring Overlook as a component of the Mount Pisgah Recreation Area. (Author's collection.)

Three

EARLY YEARS OF PISGAH NATIONAL FOREST INN

In 1899, the *Raleigh News and Observer* reported that George Farrington Weston was "a brilliant and brainy member of the Board of Agriculture; superintendent of the famous Biltmore Farm; a pleasant, amiable gentleman . . . one of the best known men in the state." Like his father, George Weston studied engineering, science, and agriculture. Around 1917, Weston built Pisgah Inn on a 2.9-acre shelf below Mount Pisgah in the new Pisgah National Forest. (Courtesy NPS/BRP.)

In the 1800s, William Weston, a barrister at the Queen's Court in England, immigrated to America. Weston's son, Thomas Aldridge Weston, an accountant, inventor, and mechanical engineer, received a patent for his invention of the differential pulley system. In the 1870s, Thomas moved to Western North Carolina for health and business purposes. Pack Memorial Library in Asheville, North Carolina, preserves his detailed scrapbook of Asheville's agricultural, business, railroad, and natural history. Near Arden, North Carolina, Thomas purchased Rock Hall, a 400-acre estate. Only remnants of the structure remain today. At Rock Hall, Thomas raised three children, George Farrington Weston, Eleanor Kate Weston, and Marianne Aldridge Weston (Ross). Calvary Episcopal Church in Fletcher, North Carolina, became the family's church home and the final resting place for Thomas Weston in 1901. (Both, courtesy Pack Memorial Library.)

Thomas Weston's only son, George F. Weston, became a skilled engineer and architect and, like his father, possessed a great knowledge and interest in agriculture. Between 1895 and 1903, he served as the superintendent of farms for George Vanderbilt's Biltmore Estate. During that period, he also served on the North Carolina Board of Agriculture. After Vanderbilt married Edith Stuyvesant Dresser in Paris in 1898, the couple arrived home at the Biltmore Village train station. On horseback, George Weston, forester Carl Schenck, and Biltmore superintendent Charles McNamee met them at the depot. Under a giant horseshoe of goldenrods, the three estate ambassadors escorted the Vanderbilts home to Biltmore. That evening, Weston led a welcoming torchlight parade for the newlyweds around the grounds of the Biltmore House. (Illustration by Ken Czarnomski; photograph courtesy North Carolina State University.)

Around 1903, George Weston left the Biltmore Estate and moved to New York. On April 19, 1912, a note tucked in the corner of the *Asheville Gazette-News*, teeming with the *Titanic*'s tragic news, announced the engagement of George Weston and Mary Cynthia Wheeler. The couple travelled regularly from New York to visit Weston's widowed mother in Fletcher, North Carolina, and moved to the area around 1917 to build their mountain inn near Mount Pisgah. After obtaining a concession permit from the US Forest Service, Weston designed and began building his Pisgah National Forest Inn around July 1919. During the construction, he and his wife camped in a tent on Pisgah Ridge for eight weeks, where "I could live for the rest of my life," Weston told a reporter. (Courtesy Library of Congress.)

"A mountain inn company is promoting the use of the national forest for recreational purposes," announced an *Asheville Citizen* article on July 19, 1919. "The camping colony is being built by George Weston and is located about two miles from the Vanderbilt lodge near Bad Branch Gap, four miles from the top of Mount Pisgah and on the famous Mount Pisgah automobile road leading into the Pink Beds of Pisgah National Forest." Weston planned to build cottages and tent-bungalows for campers who wanted "a more convenient style than by sleeping on the ground and suffering the ill effects of camping without suitable facilities." The USFS initiated programs to promote public use of Pisgah's resources and supported Weston's efforts to encourage camping and recreational activities in the new national forest. On both November 4, 1920, and May 7, 1921, USFS supervisor Verne Rhoades signed the Pisgah National Forest Inn registry and visited a newly constructed tent-bungalow. (Courtesy UNCA.)

George Weston enlisted the help of local labor to build and work at his inn. In this poor, remote region, families welcomed a steady source of income. One man walked six miles from Wady Branch, a tributary of Pisgah Creek in Haywood County, every day to help build the inn. His teenage son worked in maintenance. The rock steps that aided their steep climb from Hardy Cove to the current Mount Pisgah Recreation Area are still visible. According to historian Chet Hill, a young man raised in Cruso could look up to Pisgah Ridge from his home and see his father in a white shirt working at Pisgah Inn. Around 1919, Weston hired Montford Johnville Mease as his chauffeur. "Mountain Man" Mont Mease met visitors at the foot of the mountain on the Pisgah Motor Road (NC 151) to drive them to either Buck Spring Lodge or the Pisgah National Forest Inn. (Author's collection.)

The Pisgah National Forest Inn complex eventually included a main lodge and four separate cottages. Designed in the pine-knot architectural style popular in the Adirondacks at the time, Weston used natural materials, often leaving bark on the logs to allow the rustic buildings to blend into the natural setting. In the 1980s, the Historic American Buildings Survey of the 1919 Pisgah Inn, commissioned by the National Park Service, reported that Weston used pine logs to form the framework of the two-and-a-half-story lodge building. The grey board-and-batten exterior harmonized with the high-elevation mountain setting. Wood from the American chestnut tree, known for its straight-grained, tannic-rich, decay-resistant strength, paneled a wainscoted rustic interior in the lobby. (Both, courtesy Library of Congress.)

Guests pulled a wooden latch and string to enter the main lodge building and registered at a wall-mounted, self-serve reception desk beside the door. The high-beamed clubroom or lobby, graced with a massive, rough-stone fireplace and its split-log mantelpiece, welcomed guests to the mountain retreat. Stocked bookcases lined the walls. The lodge offered a gift shop and 11 to 12 bedrooms, some with connecting baths. Staff prepared meals in the kitchen, located northwest of the registration area. Adjoining the lobby, the dining room could seat 60–100 guests. Large casement windows provided long-range views of Pisgah National Forest and the surrounding landscape. (Courtesy Pack Memorial Library.)

Next to the chimney, a handsome staircase invited guests to the upper-level bedrooms. To design this native showpiece, craftsmen used bark-covered posts to support split-log steps in the pine-knot architectural style popular for mountain lodges. Nature's artistic handiwork provided the unique newel post to secure the handrail. George Weston also accented outdoor balconies, window moldings, the entrance portico, the exterior facade, and the cottages with this coarse, born-of-the-forest decorative motif. (Courtesy Library of Congress.)

In the early days, George Weston provided guest accommodations only on the second floor. From the southwest balcony, visitors, or possibly the cooking staff, entered two bedrooms and a bath located above the kitchen. After 1966, however, the old lodge became employee housing for Pisgah Inn staff, and the owners converted the kitchen into lodging quarters. (Courtesy Library of Congress.)

Each morning at sunrise or in the evening at the end of a leisurely paced day, visitors swung out large-paned bedroom windows, taking in a majestic view or a breath of fresh mountain air. Cedar waxwings, chestnut-sided warblers, juncos, and towhees added charm to the quiet stillness and beckoned lodge patrons on holiday to step outside for a better view. (Courtesy Library of Congress.)

The East Room and bath (a later addition to the Pisgah Inn complex) connected to the main lodge through a small hallway and had its own fireplace and exterior chimney. In the 1960s, the owners remodeled this lower-level room, like the kitchen, to provide for employee housing. In 1974, however, a fire severely damaged the East Room. (Courtesy Library of Congress.)

A wide deck with rough, natural wood railings afforded a grand, panoramic view of Black Mountain, Funnel Top Mountain, Looking Glass Rock, and the Pink Beds Valley of Pisgah National Forest. Evenings brought a peaceful stillness as the sunset's afterglow tinted the landscape in pale pink, yellow, and purple. An autumn chill and seasonal change set the mountain ridges aglow with fall colors. (Courtesy Library of Congress.)

To the left of the portico entrance of the main lodge building, stonemasons used native stones, like those used for the structure's foundation, to form a tall coarse-rock chimney, rounded at the top. Exposed log beams, like overarching, protective tree branches, supported the rooftop shelter over the inn's double-door entry. (Courtesy Library of Congress.)

The above photograph provides a closer view of the beams above the entrance doorway. In the lobby and dining room, rough-hewn chestnut posts held two log beams at 45 degrees to brace the horizontal crossbeams along the ceiling. Known in architectural parlance as the post-and-lintel system, this construction style created a spacious, airy ambience in the lobby and dining room; it was like walking among trees in an open forest. (Both, courtesy Library of Congress.)

Like the great camps of the Adirondacks, four individual cabins offered guests quiet solitude and encouraged them to commune with the natural world as they walked between the buildings of the lodge complex. On Pisgah Ridge, the Kalmia Cottage snuggled among dense thickets of mountain laurel (*Kalmia latifolia*) and its related rhododendron. Carl Linnaeus, the "father of modern taxonomy," named this shrub after 18th-century Swedish botanist Peter Kalm, who collected laurel specimens near the Hudson River. (Courtesy Library of Congress.)

Kalmia Cottage, the closest cabin to the main lodge building of the Pisgah National Forest Inn complex, also had grey board-and-batten exterior siding. This one-story cottage held two bedrooms connected by a bath, and each bedroom opened to a front porch. A corner fireplace provided heat. South-facing windows offered great views. (Courtesy Library of Congress.)

Next to the Kalmia Cottage, the one-story, elevated Chinquapin Cottage sported its board-and-batten siding under a double-gabled roof. Guests climbed the stairs to the wooden porch and entered the front door into the sitting area. A second door opened into the bedroom with a bath. A fireplace warmed cool evenings. (Courtesy Library of Congress.)

During the summers of 1969, 1970, and 1971, Carolyn Davis of Hominy Valley and her future husband, Mickey Allen, worked at the new Pisgah Inn, built in 1965, and lived in the 1919 lodge. Carolyn's father, Army veteran Ted Donald Davis (1918–1999), was a valuable resource for a busy Pisgah innkeeper. With Ted's easygoing, versatile nature, he cooked, baked, washed dishes, substituted for sick chefs, ran the gift shop, collected the mail and supplies in the inn's Volkswagen van, and worked as the inn's caretaker during the winter months. In August 1971, after Carolyn and Mickey married, they lived in the Chinquapin Cabin until the end of the working season. In 2019, they reserved an overnight stay at the inn to celebrate their 48th anniversary. (Both, courtesy NPS/BRP.)

The innkeepers named the cabin after the chinquapin tree, a species related to the American chestnut. In the early 1900s, a fungus from Asia devastated chestnut forests throughout the Appalachians. However, several young native chestnut trees still grow along Pisgah Ridge near Pisgah Inn. (Courtesy Library of Congress.)

In a long-term project to produce fungus-resistant trees, the National Park Service permitted the American Chestnut Foundation to pollinate some of Pisgah's native trees with pollen from more resistant chestnut trees in Virginia around 2004. Volunteers later collected their seeds to plant them in a seed orchard. The foundation now tends the Pisgah chestnut tree "grandchildren" and "great-grandchildren" hybrids in an orchard in Edneyville, North Carolina. (Courtesy Paul Sisco, Mark Alexander, and the American Chestnut Foundation.)

The eastern towhee, a black and copper ground-dwelling bird often heard scratching in forest-floor leaf litter, inhabits brushy areas like the rhododendron thickets on Pisgah Ridge. Its cheerful song sounds like an invitation to "Drink your tea-ee-ee!" But its spunky call note bursts out like a welcoming "Chewink!" and became the name of the cabin located at the far western edge of the Pisgah National Forest Inn complex. Guarded by gnarled oak trees and resting on a rock foundation, Chewink Cabin, a modest, L-shaped, two-bedroom cabin, shared a bath, closet, and small fireplace. Separate bedroom doors opened onto the covered front porch. (Both, courtesy Library of Congress.)

Treetops Cabin sat apart from the Kalmia, Chinquapin, and Chewink Cabins. The largest of the four rental cabins, Treetops Cabin rose high above the rhododendron bushes and the stunted tree trunks. Like the others, its weathered board-and-batten exterior blended with the elements on this high-elevation ridgeline. (Courtesy Library of Congress.)

Lodge patrons rented the spacious two-story Treetops Cabin for a night, a week, or even several months at a time. The 1920s–1930s Pisgah Inn registry records some wealthy travelers returning several times during a single summer season for an overnight stay or a gourmet dinner at the lodge restaurant. One Charleston professor returned each summer with his piano. (Courtesy Library of Congress.)

Guests entered Treetops Cabin through one of two ground-level doorways, each located at opposite ends of the building. On the west end, a small roof sheltered the entrance below the covered balcony on the second level. Note the fire escape ladder next to the balcony, bolted to the north side of the cottage. It was added in the 1970s. (Courtesy Library of Congress.)

In the 1960s, Pisgah Inn owners refurbished the roomy Treetops Cabin to accommodate employees living on-site for the summer. Partitions, updated lighting fixtures and furniture, and white-painted walls and ceilings provided a more modern—and less rustic—homelike setting. In 1979, a one-room ground-level bathroom addition improved the original, single bathroom for this large two-level cottage. (Courtesy Library of Congress.)

Treetops Cabin was located beside a water tower, which was removed before the 1980s. In the early days, a cold mountain spring located about a half-mile north of the Pisgah National Forest Inn supplied the water. A pump drove the springwater through over-the-ground pipes to the storage tower located near Treetops. Beyond the water tower, a lodge workshop later doubled as a garage. Nearby, the original laundry building later served as the laundry facility for Pisgah Inn employees. George Weston strove to accommodate the comfort needs of his guests and their unique personalities. One recurrent visitor, it is said, always travelled with her cats, but the lady thought that the other lodge patrons gave her cats too much attention. So Weston built a small, separate cabin for the dear madam and her feline companions. (Both, courtesy Library of Congress.)

"For those who have visited Pisgah Forest Inn on Mount Pisgah, the name of Mrs. George Farrington Weston will instantly recall memories of the gracious hostess who made the place famous for its cordiality," an *Asheville Citizen-Times* article fondly noted on April 1, 1934. Before coming to Pisgah, Mary Wheeler Weston completed three years of graduate studies in piano and composition at the New England Conservatory of Music in Boston. In New York, where she met George, she was an accompanist at Teachers College, Columbia University, and was the organist at Calvary Baptist Church. At Pisgah, she found artistic expression in her study of Western North Carolina wildflowers. In 1921, Mary began transplanting nearly 300 species of native plants to her one-acre garden east of the main lodge building. Today, a dense growth of rhododendrons and mountain laurels claims the site of her former garden. Snakeroot, Solomon's seal, asters, and galax peak through the leaf litter in a few scattered, sunlit areas. (Courtesy NPS/BRP.)

A friend of forest creatures, Mary Weston fed the squirrels and the birds. Just like the Civilian Conservation Corps recruits at the US Deer Farm in the Pink Beds of Pisgah National Forest (seen here), Mary would bottle-feed fawns needing her care. In 1962, a *Greensboro Daily* reporter wrote, "The sign of the inn is a deer, designed by the Westons who felt it appropriate because the area was a deer crossing." (Above, courtesy Bruce O'Connell; below, courtesy UNCA.)

Since Pisgah Inn's opening season in 1920, prominent visitors from around the globe have visited the mountain lodge. Between 1929 and 1932, visitors from Canada, England, New Zealand, Cuba, Ireland, Switzerland, Holland, France, India, and Hong Kong signed the Pisgah Inn registry. During that same period, guests arrived from 38 states. Many visited from Washington, DC. Pictured from left to right, Reuben Robertson of Champion Papers (retired); Richard Preston, dean of the School of Forestry at North Carolina State University; and Walter Damtoft of Champion Papers (retired) pose in the dining room of the Pisgah Inn on June 25, 1966. (Left, sketch by former employee Dotsie Evans; below, courtesy UNCA.)

In 1931, American Forestry Association members gathered on the front porch of the Pisgah Inn. G.A. Schulze, graduate of the Biltmore Forest School, signed the register four times in 1929, twice in 1930, and twice in 1931, listing his address as the Bureau of Plant Industry, Washington, DC. Other visitors recorded addresses from the Asheville School for Boys as well as Clemson, Bluefield, and Berea Colleges. Camp Merri-Woode, a girl's camp in Sapphire, North Carolina, that opened in 1919, also visited Pisgah Inn in the 1930s. Land of the Sky Motor Tours brought tourists from Ohio, Kentucky, West Virginia, and Pennsylvania. Some patrons signed in as husband and wife "and chauffeur." Chauncey Beadle, horticulturalist for the Biltmore Estate at the time, visited Pisgah Inn several times between September 1929 and May 1931. Was he entertaining friends or searching for another species of azalea? In 1930, Beadle became an avid collector of local azaleas, transplanting them to the Biltmore Estate. Today, the Biltmore House and Garden preserves his collection in the Azalea Garden on the estate. (Courtesy North Carolina State University.)

On May 25, 1929, author Horace Kephart, from Bryson City, North Carolina, signed the Pisgah Inn registry next to Japanese-born George Masa, from Asheville. Together, the close friends explored the southern Appalachians and helped map the Appalachian Trail through the Smokies. Like Dr. Chase P. Ambler of Asheville, who visited the Pisgah Inn on July 13 of that year, Kephart and Masa campaigned for the creation of Great Smoky Mountains National Park. After working as a

bellhop at the Grove Park Inn, Masa became a professional photographer. His artistic capture of the area's natural beauties enticed others to explore the mountainous region and prompted public leaders to protect it. From Big Bald Mountain, south of Pisgah Inn, Masa took this photograph of, from left to right, Mount Pisgah, Little Pisgah Mountain, and Little Bald Mountain. Pisgah Inn rests in the foreground. (Courtesy Pack Memorial Library.)

During its inaugural season, Pisgah Inn welcomed E.W. Grove on July 25, 1920. Grove had built Asheville's Grove Park Inn around 1913. In October 1929, Grove's son-in-law Fred Seely came to visit Pisgah Inn, a month after the inn had hosted 12 members of the Enka Holland organization. Seely had negotiated with the Dutch company's officials to establish America's largest rayon producing plant in Buncombe County, providing thousands of jobs during the Great Depression. The July 1930 edition of the *Enka Voice* reported that over a dozen Holland girls had trained approximately 1,200 Western North Carolina girls for the past year "to be efficient and dependable workers in the Hominy Valley plant of the American Enka Corporation." During their stay in America, the Dutch technicians and advisors toured Mount Mitchell, Chimney Rock, Pisgah Inn, and other tourist attractions. (Both, courtesy Pack Memorial Library.)

At Pisgah Inn, the Westons hosted prominent friends from Fletcher, North Carolina, about 11 miles west of Asheville. In 1929, Rev. and Mrs. Clarence Stuart McClellan of Calvary Episcopal Church visited Pisgah Inn several times. Jenny Westfeldt, a cousin of Overton Westfeldt Price, a forester who apprenticed under Carl Schenck at the Biltmore Estate and served as the US Forest Service assistant chief under Gifford Pinchot, also registered at Pisgah Inn. Between 1929 and 1932, Fletcher community leaders Preston L. Wright, Dr. and Mrs. Shuford, Mr. and Mrs. David Blake, Miss D. Rutledge, Mr. and Mrs. R. Walter Fletcher, Maria and Bertha Fletcher, and Edward F. Beal, Esq., from Pennsylvania, also came. George and Mary Weston lived at the inn during the summer season but stayed at Weston's birthplace home, Rock Hall, in Arden during the winter. In 1937, when Weston retired as Pisgah Inn's manager, he returned to Shenstone, a home he built in Fletcher in 1931. In 1946, at George Weston's funeral at Calvary Episcopal Church in Fletcher, North Carolina, Dr. Shuford and Overton Price's son served as pallbearers. (Courtesy Library of Congress.)

Asheville real estate developers, architects, builders, and businessmen, such as L.B. Jackson, J.M. Westall, and Tench C. Coxe, also visited the inn in the 1920s and 1930s. Frank Wolfe, brother of author Thomas Wolfe, came twice. In the 1950s, Pisgah Inn's manager told a reporter that, one Sunday, the staff served a buffet lunch to a Chinese professor at Columbia University, a couple from Germany, a former Prussian officer, and a refugee from a concentration camp. (Courtesy Pack Memorial Library.)

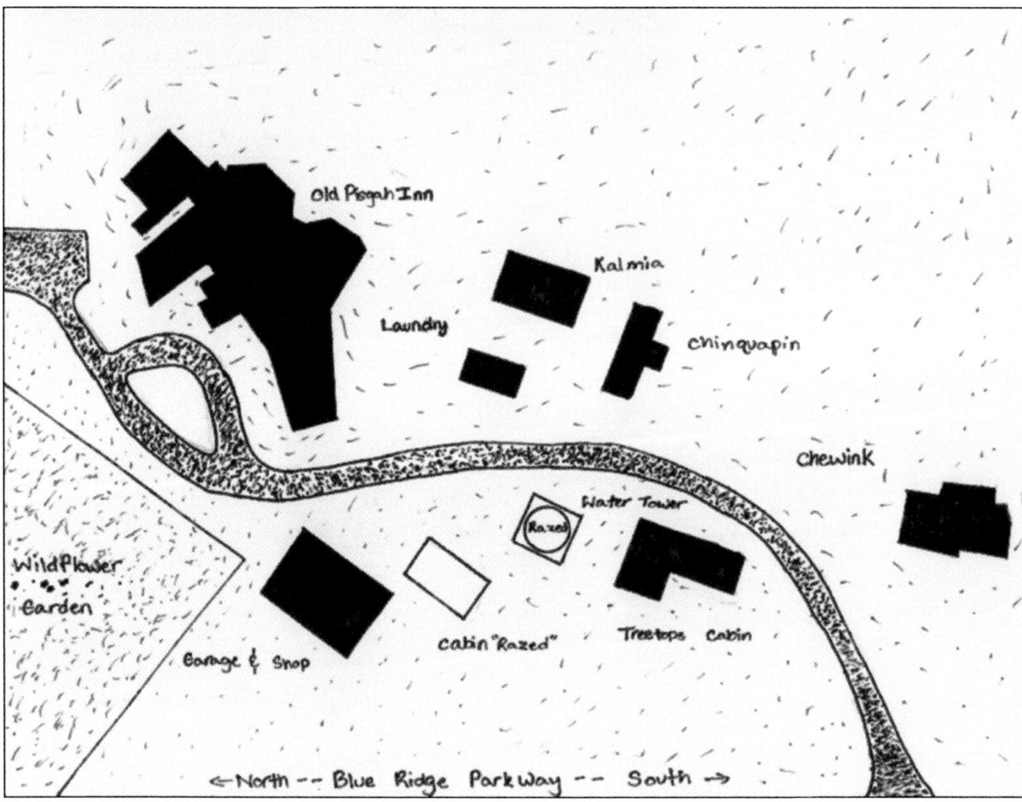

In 1937, with 12 years remaining on the 30-year forest service lease, experienced hotel administrators H.H. Nash and Harold V. Moon assumed the management of Pisgah Inn. However, World War II drastically reduced tourism. By 1948, Maurice Hess and Bess Cameron managed Pisgah Inn. Three years later, Long Island residents Leslie G. and Leda D. Kirschner responded to an advertisement, purchased the inn, and began renovations. A 1930s illustration by Nash showing the location of the original lodge buildings hangs in the inn's current Grazing Deer Café. (Illustration by Michael Worsham; courtesy Shelby and Lydia Wallace.)

Four

The Blue Ridge Parkway Brings Change

Pres. Franklin D. Roosevelt approved the construction of a scenic parkway connecting the Shenandoah and Great Smoky Mountains National Parks. On September 11, 1935, crews began building the 469-mile Blue Ridge Parkway at Cumberland Knob, near the North Carolina–Virginia line. Under the Department of Interior, the National Park Service manages this well-travelled, linear national park as well as the panoramic overlooks and recreational areas along the route. (Courtesy Library of Congress.)

An August 1937 *Asheville Citizen* article reported the sale of Pisgah Inn to Harold Moon and Harry Nash; the purchase price "was not disclosed but understood to be $27,000." However, a note attached to a December 4, 1945, letter from Blue Ridge Parkway superintendent Sam Weems to US Forest Service supervisor Carl Kruger stated that Moon and Nash rented the inn from George Weston for $2,000 a year. In their contract, Moon, Nash, and Weston agreed that any state or federal compensation received for damages to the inn caused by parkway construction belonged to Weston. Weston's original 30-year US Forest Service land lease would expire on October 1, 1949. (Both, courtesy Library of Congress.)

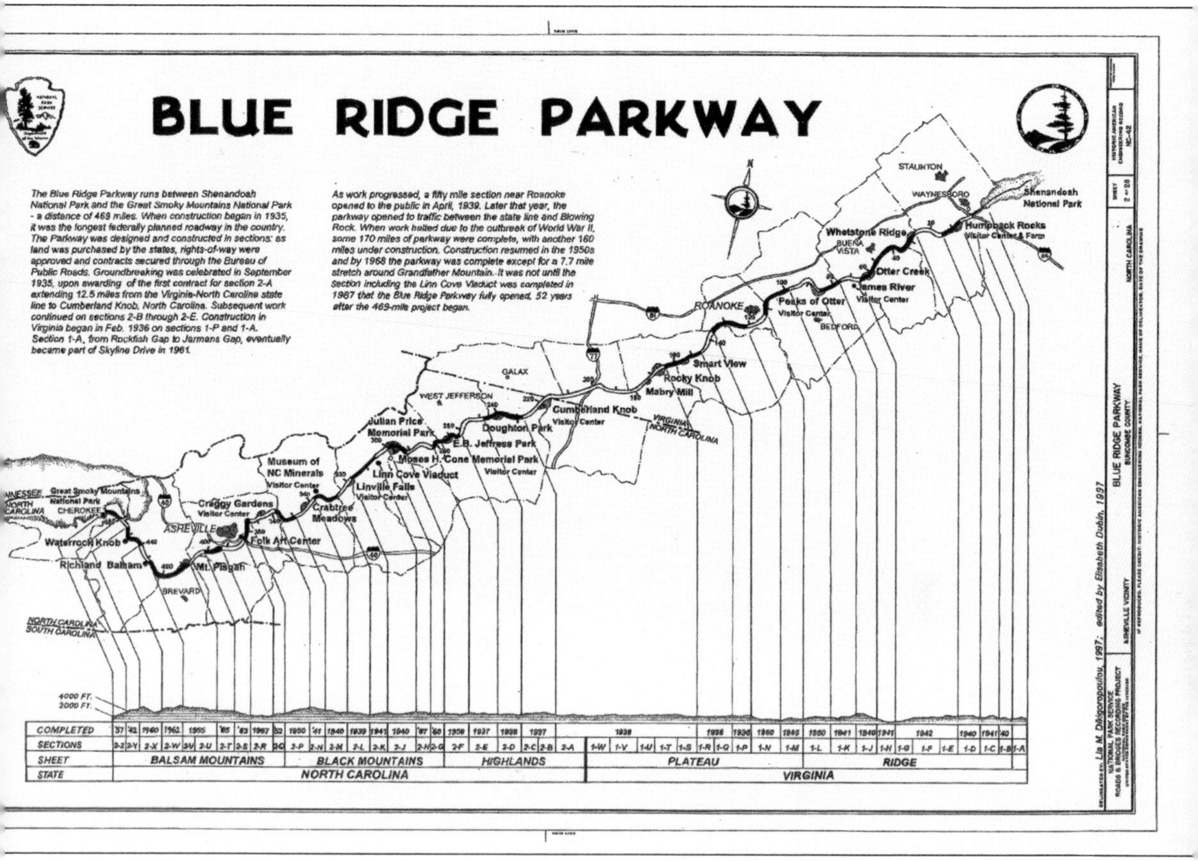

In the 1930s, the Blue Ridge Parkway landscape architects, under the direction of Supt. Stanley Abbott, began designing the route of the scenic roadway through Virginia and North Carolina. Major objectives were to enhance the motorist's visual impact and to preserve historic sites. In the 1940s, the NPS approached Pisgah Inn owners Harry Nash and Harold Moon about the anticipated changes. (Courtesy Library of Congress.)

An early proposal placed the parkway on the north side of Pisgah Ridge, requiring crews to fill in a large ravine. A later idea suggested moving the Pisgah Inn and placing the Blue Ridge Parkway along the southern edge of the ridgeline. On October 4, 1945, BRP superintendent Sam Weems wrote, "The revised line will completely wipe out the Pisgah Motor Inn, and I am inclined to believe that this is a good idea since this operation will no doubt result in an administration headache in the future." (Courtesy Library of Congress.)

After numerous discussions, BRP superintendent Sam Weems reversed his opinion. On November 6, 1951, he wrote to senior highway engineer F.W. Cron saying, "Our plans are still nebulous, but we do definitely plan a development at the Pisgah Motor Inn site. The Parkway location on the north side of the present development permits better layout for the inn and does not spoil its fine view with a road in front of the building." (Courtesy Library of Congress.)

In 1951, when Leslie and Leda Kirschner purchased the Pisgah Inn, the couple restored sections of the original inn that had fallen into disrepair. Like a master culinary artist, Kirschner prepared exquisite meals in his signature white apron and chef's hat. His charismatic wife managed the inn and directed the guest services, often charming patrons with her skilled wood-carving treasures. (Courtesy UNCA.)

In November 1957, USFS supervisor D.J. Morriss sent a letter to the Kirschners at Pisgah Inn. Their 10-year USFS land lease contract, at a $100-a-year fee plus one percent of net sales, would expire in October 1961. The USFS planned to transfer its Pisgah Inn property to the NPS for the construction of the Blue Ridge Parkway. By 1963, parkway officials planned to break ground in the Pisgah region to build roadways, overlooks, tunnels, and bridges. NPS officials presented the Kirschners with an offer—a 20-year NPS concessions contract if the couple agreed to finance and build new visitor accommodations near the original Pisgah Inn site. The park service planned to remove the original 1919 inn later. Outlined in the Blue Ridge Parkway master plan, the innkeepers had to complete the modern inn with 15 new rooms, a restaurant, a gas station, and large parking lot by 1965 and add 15 more rooms by June 1967. "The great advantage of executing the proposed contract at this time," expressed a Blue Ridge Parkway regional director, "lies in the ability to schedule concessioner construction to coincide with Parkway construction." (Courtesy UNCA.)

The Kirschners needed an estimated $250,000 to build and equip the new Pisgah Inn facility required by the park service. J. Aaron Prevost, owner of Unagusta Manufacturing Company of Hazelwood, North Carolina, found enthusiastic partners in Waynesville to join him and the Kirschners to form the investment group Pisgah Inn, Inc.—J.H. Woody, executive vice president of the First Union National Bank; John Johnson, owner of Automotive Heating Company; and businessman George K. Kimball. The USFS extended the Kirschners' special use permit until December 1962 and transferred its ownership of the Pisgah Inn property to the NPS in May 1963. Park officials would provide roads, parking areas, utilities, and signs for its new concession facility. Blue Ridge Parkway superintendent and landscape architect Stanley Abbott advocated an expansive overlook at the Pisgah Inn property, where "the view of the Pink Beds is superb, as you know." (Above, author's collection; below, courtesy Bruce O'Connell.)

"The present buildings, we believe, have outlived their usefulness," Superintendent Weems wrote to the Kirschners. "We are obliged under the NPS congressional policy to provide more modern facilities for parkway visitors." Officials temporarily allowed the 1919 Pisgah National Forest Inn structures to remain for storage and employee housing. In 1964, Pisgah Inn, Inc., and government officials signed the first 20-year NPS concession contract. Architects Foy, Lee, Moody, and Associates of Waynesville, North Carolina, designed the new inn with fieldstone, board-on-board vertical siding, large overhangs, and low-sloped roofs. Between 1963 and 1964, Howard Liner and the Haywood Contracting Company built the restaurant, gift shop, office building, and new lodge units. Inclement weather, a five-foot snowstorm, and wind-driven rains "falling up, not down," hampered the crew's progress, a family member reported. The last lodge unit constructed in 1966–1967 added 20 rooms. Pisgah Inn's service station and store opened on July 18, 1965. (Both, courtesy NPS/BRP.)

With his professional eye merging landscape design with natural and cultural elements, the 25-year-old former project organizer for the Civilian Conservation Corps Stanley Abbott became the Blue Ridge Parkway's resident landscape architect and superintendent. Defining the parkway corridor was the first step. "As we traveled through the mountains on general reconnaissance," he said, "we were guided by some sense of need for rhythm or pattern, a jewel on a string of beads occurring every so often, so there was one comprehensive plan." Today, a motorist cruises southwest of Asheville, weaving around and through mountains on the parkway—"a flowing ribbon upon the landscape"—and ascends steadily toward Mount Pisgah. Beyond Pisgah Inn, the traveler turns northwest at the parkway's most southern dip at Beech Gap (Milepost 423.2), crosses the Great Balsam Mountains and its highest peak, Richland Balsam (6,043 feet), and enters the Plott Balsam Range to complete a parkway journey at the home of the Eastern Band of the Cherokee Nation (Milepost 469). (Courtesy Library of Congress.)

When crews began building the Blue Ridge Parkway through the Pisgah region, over 20 years had passed since its construction began. World War II had interrupted its progress. To boost the public's war-weary morale and improve the nation's protected natural areas, Pres. Dwight D. Eisenhower initiated the Mission 66 Project in 1956. He allocated government funds to help rehabilitate visitor services in the national parks. In 1966, the culmination of the 10-year project would coincide with the 50th anniversary of the National Park Service. The US government funded the construction of the Blue Ridge Parkway section along Pisgah Ridge using Mission 66 dollars. (Both, courtesy NPS/BRP.)

Roughly following topographical contours, the parkway's gentle curves and sloping inclines allowed both driver and passengers to scan the natural landscapes and diverse vegetative zones along the route. Widened areas like Pounding Mill Overlook, photographed in October 1955 on Pisgah Ridge south of Pisgah Inn, offered a brief motorist stop for a relaxed, long-range view. Parkway officials notified the Kirschners at Pisgah Inn that engineers would begin building the parkway section across Pisgah Ridge between Wagon Road Gap (currently the Blue Ridge Parkway juncture with US 276) and Flat Laurel Gap near the inn. "When we start from Cutthroat Gap" [now called Elk Pasture Gap], the superintendent explained, "there will be a way to your place along the parkway from Wagon Road Gap." (Courtesy NPS/BRP.)

For the most part, architects chose not to place the parkway across a mountain's highest peak. Instead, they perpetuated the roadway's graceful, curving theme, while respecting a mountain's dignity and handsome profile, by tunneling through an adjoining side ridge. By aligning the parkway around distinctive landforms and through lower-elevation slopes, the Blue Ridge Parkway lessened the man-made impacts on the beauty and character of the natural environment. Numerous skilled contractors provided the roadway fill, slope stabilization, gravel, guardrails, grading, paving, and other services to achieve the architects' goals. (Courtesy NPS/BRP.)

Between Blue Ridge Parkway Milepost 397, near the French Broad River Bridge, and Milepost 410.1 at Fryingpan Gap, near the Pisgah Inn, motorists and cyclists duck through 10 of the parkway's 26 tunnels. Handcrafted by master stonemasons, these bold, artistic structures lend an air of underground adventure and variety to the cruising experience. (Courtesy NPS/BRP.)

Two tunnels near Pisgah Inn—the Little Pisgah Tunnel, pictured here at Milepost 406.9, and the Buck Spring Tunnel at Milepost 407.3—display the characteristic stonemasonry style of parkway tunnels, bridges, and rock walls. Like many of the parkway's gifted stonemasons, Joseph M. Troitino practiced his labor-intensive trade with boundless energy, eager enthusiasm, and steadfast commitment. Troitino's dedicated work ethic inspired his Spanish crew to build over 75 percent of the parkway's rockwork. (Courtesy Teri Troitino Connelly.)

In 1920, Joe Troitino, the teenage son of a skilled stonemason, boarded a ship in Spain bound for a more promising future in America. At a Welch, West Virginia, Catholic church construction site, supervisors quickly recognized the young Spaniard's natural skill with a hammer and a chisel and hired him. After Troitino helped build Virginia Tech in Blacksburg, Virginia, and landed his first supervisory role building a motel, his reputation as a superior artisan grew. Like the Spanish and Italian stonemasonry families of Giobbi, Redollfi, Rovere, Vecellio, Rizoti, and others, Blue Ridge Parkway officials hired stonecutter Joe Troitino in the 1930s. Based in Asheville, North Carolina, the team of Troitino and Brown built several tunnels along Pisgah Ridge. Pictured above are, from left to right, Joe Troitino, Taylor Sutton, and Nello L. Teer at the 1986 Blue Ridge Parkway dedication ceremony at Cumberland Gap. (Above, courtesy Teri Troitino Connelly; right, courtesy Library of Congress.)

Tenacious, hardworking, and attentive to detail, Joe Troitino spent 50 years selecting, hand cutting, and laying stones in masonry projects on the Blue Ridge Parkway, in the Great Smoky Mountains National Park, and in government office projects in the capital of his adopted country. In a 2003 interview at the Blue Ridge Parkway Headquarters, near Asheville, North Carolina, Joe Troitino's fellow crewmember and nephew Frank Troitino Jr. described his uncle's stonemasonry career. He also described the intricate, laborious work of all stonemasons constructing Blue Ridge Parkway tunnels. Around 1964, Joe summoned Frank to help him build the tunnels near Pisgah. "Every rock has a set dimension and must fit perfectly," Frank explained. "Most of the rocks are wider on the upper sides, which hold them in place. One key rock, which is the keystone, is laid last in the middle to hold the other rocks in place." (Courtesy Library of Congress.)

Masons preferred to quarry stones near the construction site to match the quality, color, and texture of the local landscape. Elaborate wooden beams framed the archway opening. First, the crews shaped the chosen radial rocks into an arch on the ground before placing them across the portal opening. The stone veneer capped the tunnel entrance with an artistic flair and prevented falling water and debris from dropping on a passing motorist. An interviewer asked Troitino's nephew Frank Jr. which project was Joe's favorite. "Joe would go to the next job and say, 'Boys, we have to build it as soon as possible, the best we can and I want to please the government,' " replied Frank. "So, really, I'd say he was proud from one end to the other." In 1985, parkway leaders and politicians from North Carolina and Virginia gathered at Cumberland Knob to celebrate the 50 years of hard work by the dedicated construction workers who helped build the Blue Ridge Parkway. (Courtesy Teri Troitino Connelly.)

Horizontal lines were level, even if the land gradient was not. Vertical lines were unevenly spaced. Before the age of rock-cutting saws, masons hand cut stones with punch hammers and steel wedges. The favored parkway design required masons to cut a rectangular stone twice as long as its height. (Courtesy NPS/BRP.)

Exhibits along the Blue Ridge Parkway educate the public about cultural or environmental sites and commemorate historic events, but an important marker is missing. Perhaps one day, a park service exhibit will salute the passion and patriotic pride of its stonemasons. For now, their cumulative craftsmanship serves as an enduring testament of their skilled accomplishments. (Courtesy Library of Congress.)

After the 1960s, when crews linked the parkway sections north and south of Pisgah Inn, Congressman Roy Taylor and several committee members visited the Mount Pisgah area. Local communities and tourist reviews had praised the success of the new parkway's scenic and recreational value. Congressman Taylor suggested extending the parkway to Atlanta, Georgia. Politicians and engineers studied the completed roadway map. (Courtesy NPS/BRP.)

The most logical site on the parkway route to join the 190-mile Georgia extension would be at its most southern point, Beech Gap, about 15 miles from Pisgah Inn. Conservationists, historians, biologists, and private landowners protested. The proposed route to Georgia would destroy natural treasures at Panthertown Valley, Whiteside Mountain, Bridal Veil Falls, and a portion of the Appalachian Trail. Two decades of public outcry and dwindling funds tabled the matter in 1985. Here, Congressman Roy Taylor (second from left) is pictured at Beech Gap on August 6, 1973. (Courtesy NPS/BRP.)

The ease of scenic travel along the new parkway increased the number of guests at Pisgah Inn. The old lodge was popular too. In the late 1960s, the Kirschners told park staff that the structures in the former inn complex, such as the Kalmia Cabin seen here, were a "great advantage . . . housing twenty-two employees, plus seven to twenty-two percent of the guests, some by request, others for overflow." (Courtesy Library of Congress.)

The innkeepers also hosted an occasional wedding on the old inn's open deck. By 1968, though, the park service prohibited guest services in the aging structures. Until the concessioner's contract expired on December 31, 1984, the old lodge and cabins could serve as employee housing and activity rooms. Officials, however, required many structural repairs and updated safety measures. (Courtesy Library of Congress.)

In 1968, Supt. Granville Liles required the innkeepers to upgrade the 1919 Pisgah Inn to meet current safety and structural codes. They had to rewire all the buildings, add metal fire escapes to the upper floors of both Treetops Cabin and the main lodge, and replace the old balcony railings with updated, treated lumber. The NPS required that the proprietors replace electrical heaters with gas ones, repair wooden steps and handrails, stain all the exterior siding with the parkway's signature weathered-gray color, and repaint all white trim with gray enamel. By the end of the 1971 winter season, Pisgah Inn, Inc., had to also resurface all rooftops with new asphalt shingles (color decided by the NPS), modernize the employee laundry building, add a clothes dryer to minimize the use of clotheslines, and complete other projects. (Courtesy UNCA.)

In honor of the cornerstone-laying ceremony for the Cradle of Forestry in America in Pisgah National Forest, Leslie and Leda Kirschner, proprietors of Pisgah Inn (at left in photograph), hosted an event on October 20, 1964. On the balcony of the old lodge, overlooking the Pink Beds Valley, the couple presented USFS regional forester J.K. Vessey with a copy of *Primer of Forestry* by Gifford Pinchot. (Courtesy UNCA.)

In 1966, Pisgah Inn celebrated the dedication of the reconstructed Biltmore Forest School. Attending the luncheon and posing on the veranda are, from left to right, Congressman Roy Taylor; Verne Rhoades, first Pisgah National Forest supervisor; Reuben Robertson and Walter Damtoft, Champion Fibre Company; H.C. Erikson, USFS district regional forester; Peter Hanlon, USFS North Carolina supervisor; and Gus Schulze, 1907 Biltmore Forest School graduate. (Courtesy UNCA.)

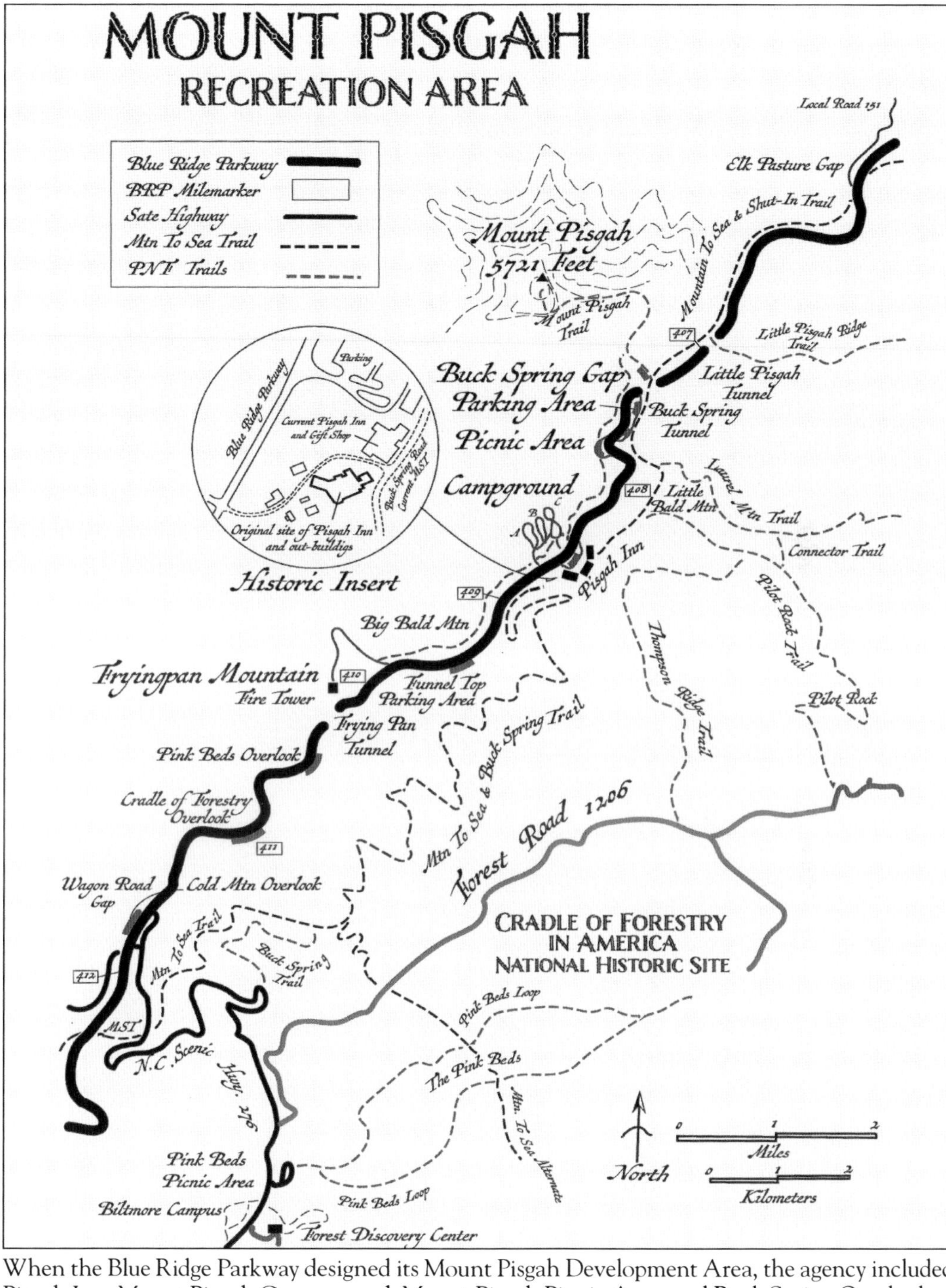

When the Blue Ridge Parkway designed its Mount Pisgah Development Area, the agency included Pisgah Inn, Mount Pisgah Campground, Mount Pisgah Picnic Area, and Buck Spring Overlook as its four component landscapes. This detailed map shows the NPS landmarks and other highlighted sites in the Mount Pisgah Recreation Area. (Courtesy Ken Czarnomski.)

Funded by President Eisenhower's Mission 66 Project, the NPS expanded the former USFS Flat Laurel Gap Campground, where Pisgah Inn owner George Weston camped with USFS supervisor Verne Rhoades in the 1920s. Mission 66 also funded the construction of a picnic ground. The four-acre Mount Pisgah Picnic Area, built on a section of Vanderbilt's former Buck Spring Lodge property, lies within the 4,920-foot contour line on the USGS Cruso Quadrangle Map. Bordering Pisgah National Forest on three sides, a grassy knob offers handicapped-accessible picnic tables, restrooms, and a view of Mount Pisgah. Rock steps and water fountains date from its 1968 construction. A former vehicle access road encircles the picnic facilities. (Above, courtesy NPS/BRP; below, courtesy UNCA.)

Around 1968, the former USFS Flat Gap Campground became the NPS Mount Pisgah Campground. Although oak, maple, birch, red spruce, hemlock, and mountain ash trees shelter an understory of rhododendron and mountain laurel, a rare, high-elevation heath bog separates the tent and trailer loops in the 74-acre campground. In March 1986, a Southern Appalachian Botanical Society article reported that the Flat Laurel Bog sediments "furnish a paleoecologic record showing vegetation change over the past 3,340 years." The NPS added more tent and trailer sites and built an amphitheater. In the 1970s, the park service provided this trailer for rangers living on-site. A 1930s registration kiosk built by the Camp Oconaluftee Civilian Conservation Corps welcomed campers at the entrance, but by 2001, a new fee-collecting building staffed by rangers greeted overnight visitors. From the 1980s to the 1990s, the Pisgah Inn managed the campground, but now the park service supervises the site. (Both, courtesy NPS/BRP.)

Like the innkeepers of Pisgah Inn over the past 100 years, visitors may see black bears, turkeys, deer, rabbits, raccoons, bobcats, and other wildlife around the Mount Pisgah Recreation Area. A former employee insisted that the recorded history of Pisgah Inn would be incomplete without honoring the notorious 10-member skunk family and its multiple black-and-white fur patterns. In tribute, a nostalgic T-shirt boasts: "I got Skunked at Pisgah Inn!" Today, wildlife-proof trash containers help deter food scavengers. Below Pisgah Inn, the historic roadway from the 1919 inn to the USFS Pink Beds is now part of North Carolina's Mountains-to-Sea Trail from Clingmans Dome to the Outer Banks and offers opportunities for wildflower and bird identification. (Left, courtesy NPS/BRP; below, courtesy Library of Congress.)

South of Pisgah Inn, a hike to the 1941 USFS Fryingpan Fire Tower affords panoramic views of the Great Balsams, the Smokies, Shining Rock Wilderness, Mount Pisgah, and the surrounding Pisgah National Forest. A two-mile trail departs the Mount Pisgah Campground, climbs Big Bald Mountain, dips into a gap (where pioneers grazed livestock and supposedly shared a communal frying pan), and ascends Fryingpan Mountain. Seen by motorists driving north or south of the inn on the Blue Ridge Parkway, the national forest's last remaining fire tower in this district is now in the National Historic Lookout Register. (Both, courtesy Dave Landreth.)

Pres. Lyndon B. Johnson's first lady encouraged Americans to plant flowers, improve public parks, and remove roadside billboards. Her Beautification Campaign created "a climate of concern about the environment," she said. "Litter, water and air pollution are problems that can be solved." In 1971, Pisgah Inn manager F. Robert Wright and his wife, Ruth, welcomed Lady Bird Johnson for an overnight stay. Ruth Wright introduced the former first lady to her dining room steward for the evening, Carolyn Davis Allen. Allen remembered serving Lady Bird a Southern specialty: country ham, grits, redeye gravy, and crème de menthe parfaits for dessert. Lady Bird and two fellow members of the advisory board for National Parks, Historic Sites, Buildings, and Monuments, retired Pennsylvania industrialist Frank Masland Jr. and Purdue University wildlife biology professor Dr. Durward L. Allen, toured national parks in Tennessee, North Carolina, and Virginia. After flying into Knoxville, visiting Cades Cove and the Great Smoky Mountains National Park, the group accompanied Blue Ridge Parkway superintendent Granville Liles on the drive from Cherokee to the Pisgah Inn. An August 5, 1971, *Asheville Citizen-Times* article announced: "Former First Lady visits Mile-high Pisgah." The Blue Ridge Parkway "is marvelous," she told reporters. "Twelve million persons are able to see these sites and enjoy them in an unhurried manner." (Courtesy Library of Congress.)

While visiting the Pisgah Inn in 1971 and signing autographs for a number of guests, Lady Bird Johnson mentioned her first trip to Western North Carolina. In March 1967, she visited a Jackson County school to support the Teachers Corps, attended a dedication ceremony for a new addition to Hunter Library at Western Carolina University, and made a surprise visit to the Thomas Wolfe Memorial in Asheville. On a bus trip to Asheville-Buncombe Technical College and Lee Edwards High School (now Asheville High School), Lady Bird Johnson is pictured here with North Carolina governor Dan K. Moore's wife and her traveling companions. When Lady Bird Johnson's group departed Pisgah Inn and the Western North Carolina area in 1971, they toured Cape Hatteras and the Wright Brothers Monument on North Carolina's Outer Banks before leaving for Virginia. (Courtesy Ewart Ball III.)

Beginning in 1965, forty-one-year-old Frank R. "Bob" Wright, a native of Vermont, managed Pisgah Inn for 12 years until his death in 1977. That year, retired corporate attorney Phyllis O'Connell and her husband, Tom, answered a *Wall Street Journal* advertisement for seasonal innkeepers at Pisgah Inn. Both were experienced hotel proprietors—Phyllis once owned the eight-story Chateau Frontenac Hotel in Detroit, Michigan, and the couple previously owned and managed the Bay Shore Royal Hotel in Tampa, Florida, and other hotels. Around 1978, the O'Connells joined Aaron Prevost and his partners to form Parkway Inn, Inc. After studying social work at Florida State University and, like Tom O'Connell, receiving a college degree in hotel administration from Cornell Hotel School, Bruce O'Connell joined his parents at Pisgah Inn. His parents had raised him in hotels. Bruce was staffing reception desks at age nine, sweeping parking lots and stairways by age 10, and at times operating Otis elevators. (Both, courtesy Bruce O'Connell.)

Innkeepers Tom and Phyllis O'Connell spent a lifetime in guest hospitality services. "My husband just kept buying me hotels," chuckled 96-year-old Phyllis during a September 2019 lunch at Pisgah Inn after her weekly drive from her Waynesville home. Beginning in 1978, Phyllis, Tom, and son Bruce shared the hotel management duties. Phyllis, the bookkeeper, organized the front office and staffing assignments. Tom handled housekeeping and maintenance projects, and Bruce managed the food service. (Courtesy Bruce O'Connell.)

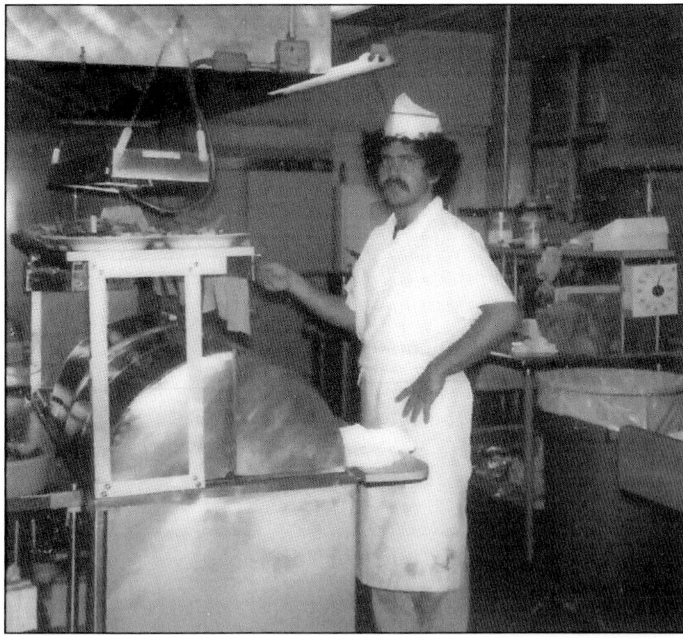

From the 1960s to the 1980s, an employee affectionately known as "Aunt Bea" shared renovated living quarters in the 1919 Pisgah Inn buildings with younger staff members, some of whom were college students working during their summer break. When she settled in her room at the end of a busy day, Aunt Bea would knock on her bedroom wall if the music got too loud. "Sometimes they paid attention and sometimes they didn't," she told a reporter. (Courtesy Bruce O'Connell.)

In 1965, the year that construction crews completed Project Section 2U of the Blue Ridge Parkway through the Pisgah area, Bea Anderson came to work at the inn. Each summer, "Aunt Bea" travelled from her home in Portland, Maine, to filet the best trout, flip the tastiest pancakes, and bake the most mouthwatering cobblers "this side of the Smokies," reported a Hendersonville newspaper. One family of 12 drove 25 miles from Asheville every Saturday for her pancakes. "As round as she is tall with blue eyes that twinkle mischievously through her spectacles," the reporter wrote in 1985, "Bea celebrated her 73rd birthday and her 20th year at the inn." In a 1979 *Asheville Times* article, the journalist quoted the new innkeepers, Phyllis and Tom O'Connell, as saying, "She's the house mother of the staff." (Courtesy Bruce O'Connell.)

The three O'Connells operated the inn until the end of the 1984 season. Each year, when Pisgah Inn closed for the season, young Bruce worked at ski resorts during the winter. In 1985, when Tom unexpectedly passed away, former routines and professional obligations changed. The year-round responsibilities of running Pisgah Inn fell to Bruce. Phyllis, in her 60s at the time, helped manage the inn and even today, at age 96, remains engaged in the inn's operations. In 1996, Phyllis O'Connell married Aaron Prevost. He passed away in 2002. Pictured above are Phyllis and Bruce O'Connell in 2019 at the Pisgah Inn. (Photograph by the author.)

In the Mount Pisgah Recreation Area, park rangers provided visitor assistance and security. At the campground, the NPS offered interpretive programs. Here, Ranger Willie McDaniels is providing travel information to Pisgah Inn visitors on August 6, 1973. "I share much of their philosophy to protect the environment," said innkeeper Bruce O'Connell. In February 1999, he joined 36 NPS concession specialists in a training workshop at their "practice laboratory"—the Pisgah Inn. (Courtesy NPS/BRP.)

"Pisgah Inn initiated a self-imposed mandate for the 21st century to become an environmental leader," wrote Bruce O'Connell in his journal *The Last Resort, A Memoir from an Innkeeper.* "We plan to make Pisgah a model for similar businesses. Watch us turn green right before your eyes in the next few years." Passionate about climate change, recycling, and air pollution, O'Connell began initiating earth-friendly projects to reduce costs, conserve energy, and protect the environment in the 1980s. Electric cars replaced V-8 engines emitting greenhouse gasses. Dual-flush toilets reduced water waste in guest bathrooms. By 1999, energy-efficient, longer-lasting fluorescent bulbs lit 100 percent of the inn. By rerouting bathroom plumbing over hot-water heaters, O'Connell raised the temperature of the cold mountain water by 15 degrees. The pipes in the bathroom no longer dripped from condensation, and the office above the water heaters required less air-cooling energy. (Courtesy NPS/BRP.)

By 2001, solar panels heated water for the kitchen and tankless water heaters provided instant hot water for the guest rooms. Bruce O'Connell converted several vehicles to run on diesel fuel and the oil from cooking french fries. Pisgah's food delivery truck made Pisgah Inn its last stop of the day so it could recycle the inn's cardboard waste. Barbed wire and chain-link fencing keep bears from invading recycling bins for glass, plastic, and aluminum. (Courtesy Bruce O'Connell.)

In 1978, the O'Connells found George Weston's early logbooks, which recorded visitors who had returned often. For 100 years, Pisgah Inn visitors, like Tommy Morgan, migrated back to the resort. As a child, Morgan's family drove from Apex, North Carolina, for meals at Pisgah's restaurant. On August 5, 1978, he drove to Pisgah with his new wife in a dense fog. For $20, he said, they honeymooned "on the edge of the ridge in an old three-bedroom cabin with a claw-foot tub." (Courtesy NPS/BRP.)

In November 1972, after inspectors evaluated the original Pisgah Lodge buildings, NPS concessions specialist Erwin Cort informed Blue Ridge Parkway superintendent Granville Liles that the structures, valued at $12,500, had a "remaining useful life of ten years." By 1984, the O'Connells and Parkway Inn, Inc., had acquired a new 20-year NPS contract through a public bidding process. In the lease agreement, parkway officials required the concessioner to remove the worn, unsafe Pisgah Lodge and cabins. The structures have "gradually deteriorated over the years," Blue Ridge Parkway superintendent Gary Everhardt told reporters in 1987. "It's been added onto and subtracted from, patched and fixed and replaced," said Phyllis O'Connell, president of Parkway Inn, Inc. "There's very little of the original inn left." (Both, courtesy Library of Congress.)

Historic preservationists, cultural resource organizations, and the sentimental public campaigned to save the 1919 Pisgah Inn, an early chapter in the history of Pisgah National Forest and a treasured Western North Carolina 1900s architectural icon of rustic mountain lodges. Many became involved in public meetings, architectural evaluations, brainstorming sessions about restoration alternatives, cost analysis studies comparing renovation ideas, and an NPS–led tour and open house at the old inn site. Bruce O'Connell, general manager of Pisgah Inn, voiced his support to "pursue every possible avenue" to try to save it. With the parkway's inherent theme to preserve the region's natural and cultural history, park officials regretted losing a resource that was eligible for listing in the National Register of Historic Places. (Courtesy Charles Shumolis.)

Restore or remove, replace or renovate. Stabilize weakened foundations. Remove the sagging additions on the original lodge but preserve the main core. Should the whole complex be demolished and rebuild a modern lodge using the historic design? Why not upgrade the original lodge as an NPS visitor center or preserve a cabin as a museum? The bottom-line reality boiled down to economics. NPS funds fell short of the estimated $150,000 to $900,000 price tag to undertake the project. Private and public funding stalled. "Everyone wants to save it," reported a parkway official, "but when you ask how much can you contribute, interest evaporates." In June 1990, Foy, Lee, Moody, and Associates and Parkway Inn, Inc., began accepting sealed proposals from contract bidders for the demolition of the old Pisgah Inn and its associated buildings. (Courtesy Library of Congress.)

Around 1990, construction crews built new dormitories to house 60 seasonal employees at Pisgah Inn. By 2000, they added maintenance buildings near the old lodge site. Today, the 51–guest room Pisgah Inn complex invites guests for a meal, an overnight stay, or a just a scenic view. After a competitive bidding process, the NPS awarded Bruce O'Connell and his mother, Phyllis, a 10-year concessioner's contract in 2004 and again in 2014. In a partnership with the park, a concessioner pays a fee to lease government property for a privately owned business. The NPS's contractual agreement requires the concessioner to maintain established standards, make improvements, and accept the government's approval for meal prices, room rates, and other fees. Like the original 1919 Pisgah National Forest Inn, the current Pisgah Inn is tethered to the edge of Pisgah Ridge like a hang glider waiting to be free to sail over the mountainous landscape of Pisgah National Forest. (Photograph by Dave Landreth.)

Like Leda Kirschner, who introduced regional handiwork to visitors in the 1950s, Pisgah Inn continues that tradition today. Local musician Ray Pressley handcrafted walnut courting dulcimers. On a double keyboard dulcimer, a young couple faced one another to play tunes like "Go Tell Aunt Rhody," but when the music stopped, the girl's father appeared! Orin Wilkie made clocks with boards from old barns. Lewis Holloway carved wood, and Nancy Fargo decorated pottery with curved laurel handles. Local paintings, handmade jewelry, ceramics, and books are available in the current gift shop. (Courtesy Pack Memorial Library.)

About 20 percent of Pisgah Inn's workforce returns the following season. Veterans, retirees, workers in between jobs, adventure seekers, or those who just love the place reapply. Some live in the dorms; others commute. Beginning in 1970, Western Carolina University student Charles Shumolis was a busboy, waiter, and office clerk for seven seasons. Busboys, he said, lived in the original inn's kitchen. The maids commuted from Cruso. Shumolis saw a full lunar eclipse from the original inn's balcony, nearly stumbled into a bear one night, and watched "storms dropping in the valley." (Courtesy Charles Shumolis.)

"I can't imagine a more scenic drive on your way to work or a more beautiful place to spend your day," said one busboy who commuted from Asheville. "You meet interesting people from around the world," chatted a charming waitress. "Returnees" start contacting Pisgah Inn in January, said Bruce O'Connell. A Pisgah desk clerk returned seasonally for 15 years, left for a "real job," then came back. In 2019, Chris Bartholomew called O'Connell to reapply after working elsewhere for 25 years. From 1982 to 1995, he had worked at Pisgah Inn, living in the old Treetops Cabin for nearly 10 years. Bartholomew left in 1995 and helped Universal Life Ministries serve the homeless in Hawaii until the 2018 volcanic eruption destroyed access to its base camp. So Bartholomew left Hawaii and headed home to Pisgah. (Author's collection.)

Working at Pisgah Inn can be a multigenerational commitment. In the 1920s, Amy Grogan Coy's grandmother Nina Burnette Grogan (1907–1993) worked as a hostess, waitress, and maid. With her outgoing, charming personality, Nina enjoyed meeting wealthy patrons from across the globe and adored the women's fashionable attire. Nina's father, James "Jimmie" Burnette, helped build the 1919 inn, and her brother Ora Burnette worked in maintenance. As a high school student in the 1980s, Amy accepted her first job at the inn, driving the curvy road each summer from Henson Cove in Haywood County to the parkway and Pisgah Inn. As a housekeeper, she remembered cleaning the lady manager's room on the second floor of the old inn. Once, a Florida couple left her a memorable tip—a pound of bacon, a dozen eggs, a loaf of bread, and butter. "Thanks for taking care of us, Amy," their note read. "Enjoy a breakfast on us!" Pictured here are Henry Jesse and Nina Burnette Grogan. (Courtesy Amy Coy.)

After a busy summer and a slight September lull, October erupts. Food production stops. Chlorophyll breaks down. Greens fade while reds, yellows, and all the colors in between sweep across the Western North Carolina mountains. Parkway motorists find heart-stopping views of autumn's artistic displays across Pisgah National Forest from Pisgah Inn's panoramic view. (Courtesy Bruce O'Connell.)

In October, visitation triples. Guests have booked accommodations months in advance, and the dining staff serves over 1,200 people a day. Then, it stops. "Imagine traveling 200 mph in a racecar then coming to a dead stop," wrote Bruce O'Connell. "It happens on October 31 each year." Mesmerized by autumn's hypnotic spell, travelers ask, "Why do you close at the end of October?" (Courtesy Bruce O'Connell.)

The unpredictable weather at the 5,000-foot elevation can cause unexpected challenges for travelers. The freeze-and-thaw phenomenon caused by seasonal changes in temperature can crack rocks and dislodge large boulders. Strong winds topple trees. Landslides block roadways. Some historic weather events, like the May 8, 1992, storm at Pisgah Inn, leave lasting memories. Pictured is the snow-covered Blue Ridge Parkway at Gillespie Gap in 1977. (Courtesy NPS/BRP.)

That May morning in 1992, maintenance crews mowing the lawn reported snow flurries. An afternoon dusting of snow and 32 degrees Fahrenheit became a foot of snow by the next morning. In three days, 60 inches of snow wrapped the high ridge in a thick white blanket. The storm stranded a hotel full of guests, interrupted electrical power, closed the Blue Ridge Parkway, and disrupted Duke University botany excursions. Some travelers called their employers to report work schedule delays. This photograph shows another snow at Pisgah Inn in January 2015. (Photograph by Dan Weemhoff.)

Multiple media outlets and shows like National Public Radio and *Good Morning America* covered the unique May 1992 snowstorm. Snow showers can also occur by the end of October, when Pisgah Inn closes for the season, but November brings strong northwest winds, below-zero temperatures, and icy conditions. Like native black bears, Pisgah Inn hibernates for the winter season. This image shows a snowstorm in January 2015 at Pisgah Inn. (Photograph by Dan Weemhoff.)

When the Pisgah Inn tourist season ends for the year, winterizing begins. The staff members clean the kitchen equipment, turn the machinery off, repair shingles and leaks, tidy the guest rooms, and close the doors. They drain all the water pipes, blast the lines with an air compressor, load the system with antifreeze, and do it all again. When the work is done and the workers leave, the silence is palpable. "You could hear a leaf rolling across the parking lot," said Bruce O'Connell. "Another year full of change and delight. What say we do it again next year? Maybe, we can improve—make things even better for you and the environment." This winter scene shows the Blue Ridge Parkway's Craggy Tunnel in 1957. (Courtesy NPS/BRP.)

Bibliography

Asheville Citizen. "Biltmore Ranger Killed by Huntsman." November 4, 1910.

———. "Will Build Hotel and Camp on a Site near Mt. Pisgah." July 19, 1919.

Asheville Citizen-Times. "Society, Concessionaire to Study Saving Old Inn." December 12, 1987.

"Blue Ridge Parkway." Document: HAER No. NC-42. Asheville, NC: National Park Service/Blue Ridge Parkway Archives, no date.

Coyle, Phillip E. Interview of Buck Spring Lodge historians George Cecil and William Cogburn Jr. Asheville, NC: National Park Service/Blue Ridge Parkway Archives, September 28, 2006.

———. Interview of stonemason Frank Troitino. Asheville, NC: National Park Service/Blue Ridge Parkway Archives, June 30, 2003.

Earnhardt, Jean A. "Peace and Privacy of Remote Mountain Areas Offered by Pisgah National Forest Inn." *Greensboro Daily*, July 29, 1962.

"National Park Service Cultural Landscapes Inventory, Blue Ridge Parkway: Pisgah Inn, Mount Pisgah Picnic Area, Mount Pisgah Campground, Buck Springs Overlook." Asheville, NC: National Park Service/Blue Ridge Parkway Archives, 2005.

O'Connell, Bruce. Innkeeper at Pisgah Inn. Several interviews. June–October 2019.

"Pisgah National Forest Inn (Old Pisgah Inn), Photographs: Written Historical and Descriptive Data." Document: HABS No. NC-356. Historic American Buildings Survey, National Park Service. Asheville, NC: National Park Service/Blue Ridge Parkway Archives, no date.

Pisgah National Forest Inn Registries, documenting guest signatures and visitation dates. 1929–1932. Archived by Bruce O'Connell, innkeeper/owner of Pisgah Inn.

Pless, Page. *Pisgah National Forest Inn: An Historic Review*. Manuscript. Asheville, NC: National Park Service/Blue Ridge Parkway Archives, April 27, 1982.

Schenck, Carl Alwin. *The Biltmore Story*. St. Paul, MN: Minnesota Historical Society, 1955.

Visual Character of the Blue Ridge Parkway: Virginia and North Carolina. Washington, DC: National Park Service, 1997.

Weems, Samuel, et al. Letters, documents, notes and memorandums regarding the construction of the Blue Ridge Parkway and its effect on the Pisgah Inn. Asheville, NC: National Park Service/Blue Ridge Parkway, 1945–1973.

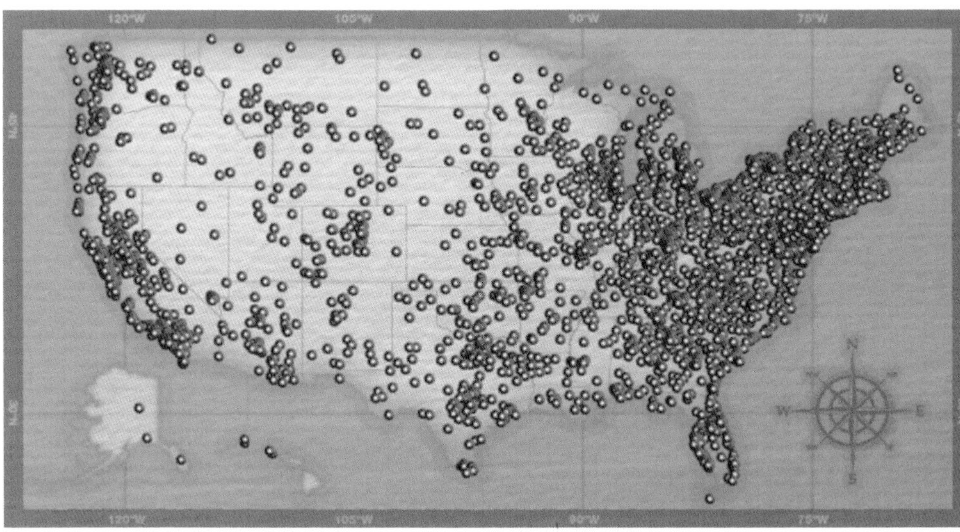